Bits
& Pieces
of a BROKEN HEART

Bits
& Pieces
of a BROKEN HEART

A Collection of Letters, Poems, and Speeches

jANiCE aNGeLa BuRT

Bits & Pieces of a Broken Heart: A Collection of Letters, Poems, and Speeches by Janice Angela Burt

Copyright © 2013 by Janice Angela Burt

For more information, visit www.spanishjanice.com

ISBN 978-0-9899125-1-8

LCCN 2013915834

Cover design & interior graphics by Marla Thompson, Edge of Water Designs, www.edgeofwater.com

Interior design by Williams Writing, Editing & Design, www.williamswriting.com

Contents

Preface

This book is a compilation of letters, poems, and speeches that I have written during the last three years. They express my thoughts and my emotions through a very difficult transition period of my life. I never had any intention of writing a book, but it occurred to me that, in all reality, I had already written one of sorts during this three-year period. One day, I sat down at my computer and started printing out all the documents that were significant to me. As I finished and looked down at my printer, there in front of me was a stack of papers about the size of a small book. I am still astounded when I think about how this writing came to be.

My purpose in publishing this book is twofold.

The first, and most important, is to speak my truth. I have done a lot of repressing and living in denial, and I want to break that cycle in a powerful way.

The second is to be fully authentic. I used to beat myself up a lot about my "humanness." In other words, all of the human emotions I would feel such as anger, sadness, jealousy, etc. were met with so much judgment on my end. However, I'm learning that those emotions are there for a reason. They are pointing me toward something within me that needs to be examined. So now, instead of ignoring them or beating myself up over them, I allow myself to fully experience them, learn from them, and then grow. In acceptance, there is the possibility for change. In judgment, there is not.

My highest hope is that my words, my struggles, my cries, and my pleas resonate with you on some level and that you will find hope and encouragement in the struggles that you face.

Welcome into my heart.

Acknowledgments

I would like to thank:

The Divine in me. I still have no words for it, but there it is.

My brother, for never really having to say he loves me because he shows it to me so well. Although he's awesome and does both!

My Cousin, for truly walking through the storm by my side.

My hypnotherapist and friend, Alicia O'Hara, for imparting her wisdom and guidance to me at such a crucial time in my life.

Asher, for the love, the years, and the lessons. And most importantly, for our two absolutely perfect children. I will always love you.

My mom and dad, for showing me the beauty and the struggle of life.

My extended family, for being magnificent, each of you, in your own unique ways.

My friends, for the companionship, the laughter, the

listening ears, and the much-needed hugs. You know who you are.

And lastly, I would like to thank life, for being my teacher, and continually propelling me to new heights.

Thank you all from the deepest part of my heart.

Special Thanks

A very special THANK YOU to those who backed my book project on Kickstarter.

Your generosity encourages, uplifts, and inspires me. This demonstration of your love and support for me will never be forgotten or taken for granted. I am so honored to share this book with you.

Amanda Bryant	Karl Styrsky	Phil Dupont
Bianca Noelle	Kate Perez	Rachel Burt
Christina Love	Kate Styrsky	Rachel Guinn
Clare Narquis	Lou Anne Merriam	Rhonda Merrill
Dave Kline	Ludid Ryu	Ron Burt
Gina Gray	Luis Garcia	RosaLee Hagstrom
Jaione Ezkerra	Malea Heim	Sarah Kabli
Jenny Swanson	Marisa Manak	Stephanie Chandler
Joanna McDowell	MegHuntress	Sue Shearer
Joel Littau	Megan Foster	Dalrymple
Jose Di Gregorio	Michelle Fox	Thomas Ladage
Karen Nelson	Nathan Carter	Tonja Field
Karl W. Palachuk	Nicole Cleveland	Tony C. Gentile

Bits
& Pieces
of a BROKEN heart

The Novel

i f you were to go out today and pick up a novel, you could happen to get one about the story of a little girl. It could be about this little girl who moved to Mexico City at the age of eight with her missionary family. You could read about how this girl was immersed in the Spanish language and culture, and loved every second of it, and how she lived there for five years before coming back to California.

You could read a chapter about this little girl becoming a teenager, and about her absolute shock and devastation when she learned that her missionary father, who preached about purity and adherence to the Bible's precepts, was actually gay and very skilled at living a double life.

You could flip the page and find out that she married her high school sweetheart, her one and only love, when she was twenty, and how they led church groups and Bible studies and how all along how very, very frightened she was by life, by love, by loss. You could skip ahead and see how her husband went from being a fundamentalist Christian, to an agnostic, to an atheist, and how this once little girl, then teenager, and now wife and mother didn't know which way to go, which way was up.

You could read on about how she gave up her own soul to please her husband, to feel the validation and approval she so desperately needed, about how she lost herself so completely in that place and about how fear dominated her every step. You could get to the page that talked about the year of counseling, the tears, and the panic attacks. And then you could get to the part where the pain she felt was worse in the place where she was than in choosing the scary unknown, and when she was finally able to let go of her childhood love.

You could keep reading about her slow journey of rediscovering herself, healing herself, and recreating herself. And there would be so much more you could read about: laughter, travels, betrayals, tears, adventures, and love all interwoven into this novel. You could pick up a novel about it or I could just tell you about it over coffee sometime, because this is a brief version of the story of my life so far.

My name is Janice Burt, and I am so honored to be a part of this Toastmasters group. I've always loved talking. When I was younger, I was given the nickname Chatterbox, if that tells you anything. So, I've always had this love for talking, and then after I lived in Mexico, I had this second love for the Spanish language. Perfectly enough, in college I majored in Spanish and minored in Communication Studies. Then I took a big chunk of time off doing any kind of professional work and focused on raising my two kids.

A year ago I passed the state test and became a court-certified Spanish interpreter. I have loved every second working in this field. It doesn't feel like work, just a lot of fun and a lot of being on my toes, of never knowing what's coming next. About six months ago, I began pursuing voice-over work. For those of you that don't know what this means, it's basically any kind of voice that you hear (on TV, radio, internet, audio books) where you don't see a face, you just hear the voice. Up until now, I've done two paid-for video promo gigs (both in Spanish) and am working on my first audio book (*Managed Services in a Month* by Karl Palachuk) in English! It also has been a blast, and I love everything about it.

It sounds like I'm good then, right? Doing two things that I absolutely love while raising my kids, how awesome is that? The thing is I have this thing, right here in my gut, that is drawing me, pulling me toward public speaking. And it's not to make money and it's not to hear myself talk. No, it's because my whole life I've been someone else's voice. My voice has merely been a reflection of what I've been told to conform to, of pleasing others, and of getting their validation. Even in my work, I interpret for others and say exactly what they say, or I read a script that someone else wrote.

But at the end of the day, I, Janice, have something to say. The thoughts are still jumbled around in my head and I'm still trying to make sense of them all, but I know that as long as I take the first step, which was joining this group, the rest will fall into place. What I don't know is how my book, this story of my life, is going to end. However, one thing I know for certain. Somehow and in some way, I will find my own voice and I will learn how to use it.

My first Toastmasters icebreaker speech.

Don't Rock the Boat

You say it's my fault that you're like this:
Miserable, stressed, unhappy.
You feel like a house slave,
Emasculated and confined.
You say the grass is greener,
You say your back is broke.
I don't want to blame, but honestly I go back . . .
Back to bitterness and resentment.
Thinking what's happening now is because
    I've never been able to put my foot down
    in the past.
And now I see why.
It hurts. Like hell.
To have a differing opinion, to feel a different
    way.
Than you.
Don't rock the boat, 'cause you'll go
    overboard. You will drown for sure.
I see there is some truth to that statement
    now.
I so desperately need you.
I just want to be free from this feeling.

Desperation

I so long to feel your loving touch again.
What do I have to do to get it back?
The tighter I hold, the more desperately
unappealing I become.
So the answer is to let you go?
Perhaps that has been the answer all along,
but I've been too scared to do it.
What if you never come back?

Twisting, spinning, slipping, sliding,
fucking a mess up in my head.
Life is becoming too much to bear. Over
what?
Stupid shit. Shit that if I wasn't so fucked
up in the head would be fairly simple
to navigate.
Instead it's all chaos, my thoughts.
It's his fault, it's my fault, it's your fault, it's
our fault.
Who the fuck cares anyway?
Life fucking sucks right now and no one
knows or cares, except he and I.

They would only care if shit came out into
    the light.
They would care enough to judge and say,
    "I told you so"
and then off they would go . . . into their
    happily-ever-after lives.
I just feel so desperate. Desperate to think,
    act, and feel differently.
Why the fuck am I not changing enough?
Being happy feels so foreign. I was at one
    time a happy person, wasn't I?
Or did I just dream that up?

A Liar

A liar, me.
Too scared to see.
Messed up and confused.
Where to look for help?
No one can help me now.
Too many thoughts,
Opinions differ at every turn.
I am wrong. I am right.
Roll the dice. Flip a coin.
I know I hurt you.
My fear causing you deep pain.
How can fright cause one to be so cruel?
Unintentionally cruel.
How could I not see the damage?
The broken pieces I would leave behind.
I need to feel pain and hurt.
In this place, I will heal.
In the scariest of places is where I will
     be set free.
Now, to bleed.

Changing the Dynamic

It's useless to wipe away the tears.
More only replace the ones that fall.
The hardest thing I'll ever say
Is swirling in my head.
The hardest thoughts, the toughest words,
As I sit here on our bed.
Our whole relationship I've held you tight,
Squeezing, suffocating out the life.
I have to change the dynamic,
Do something different.
It's always you who makes a change,
Takes the initiative.
My turn has come at last.
I'm freeing you from my grasp.
Go! Experience life!
All you've ever wanted and dreamed of is
    at your fingertips.
I no longer expect anything from you
    sexually.
I no longer will look to be validated by you.
I desire only your happiness,
Just as I continue working on mine.

To Be Free

To be free . . .
What might it feel like to be free?
Soaring over mountaintops, the
    weight of the sack of shit gone.
Stretching and flipping
Light, light as a feather
I fly.
No end in sight.
No roadblock, no fear.
It's all clear and blue and warm.
The sack of shit, I've dropped it
Somewhere, somehow.
And it's a relief like no other,
A joy and a peace.
An acceptance of myself.
It's a vision still, but I feel the sack of
    shit loosening its grip.
The chains are weakening.
Its power diminishing.
Why won't it just fall off now?
I long to be free.

The Day We Said Goodbye

To release, to fully let go.
Part torture, part relief.
So many tears, saying goodbye to my love.
The one I thought would be my forever love.
Sadness, yet peace.
Heartbreaking sobs, gut-wrenching loss.
I feel it deep down in my soul.
It is done.
Our life together is no more.
Laid to rest after so much struggle.
Where did we go wrong, my love?
What more could we have done?
To right the wrongs.
I can't look at a single picture or read a
    single letter.
It tears me up inside,
Unsettles me to the core.
Wait! Don't leave! Come back!
And tears and tears,
A fountain of sadness and loss.

Unleash This Pain

So many tears, will they ever stop, ever stop?
The pain I feel is enough to merit blood.
But I look down and all I see is the beating of
     my heart.
And I know it's calling out your name.
Yet I know I can't see you. I can't reach out.
The once familiar becomes foreign.
A stranger's face when once it was all I knew.
That face was once all I ever wanted.
And to think that I don't even know you
     anymore.
And I cry and cry and it never stops.
Tears fall and each represents a memory.
A time with you. I stand still with you.
Unleash this pain, digging deep,
Feeling what was once too painful.
I am the bird and you are the fish.
We see each other, but can't live in the other's
     world.
Impossible, tragic, a crime.
My one true love
Gone
Forever.

Placing the Blame

How did I get so lost? I ask myself so many times. The thoughts and questions are never-ending, and I want answers. I try to blame you and yes, I believe you do deserve a lot of the blame, but blaming doesn't help because you are a good soul and I see your mistakes as just that: mistakes. You got lost along the way and I followed, reluctantly and resentfully, but I followed. At the end of the day, it pulled us apart. When I really think about it, that was probably where the change should have started. Me somehow figuring out how to detach from you, to destroy the codependency, that sick and deadly disease, that horrible desperation.

The sexuality issue is what killed us. It just makes sense that sexuality would be the thing that I had to deal with in my marriage since it's always been the biggest obstacle in my life. I know you tried to include me in your sexual life and did so out of a loving place, but I never wanted and will never want to live and engage in sexuality the way you view it. I believe your view of sex is rotten. It became so at an early age, but it kept its hold on you throughout life.

You tried to shake it and change when you told me about the hidden porn addiction, but all you really did was force me to be a part of it. You spent countless hours lecturing me on sexuality and on how I viewed it all wrong. You told me countless times how sex-negative I was and how that was such a burden on you. Now I realize that my sexuality is perfectly fine and beautiful, and that it doesn't have to look like yours, and in fact, I don't want it to look like yours.

Not only that, but there is this place in you that believes come hell or high water, you are right. You convinced yourself at an early age that being right gave you validation and affirmation, in the same way that I clung to people and pleased them to receive the same. You were not an easy person to live with. You fought to the death for the things you wanted. And you did succeed. I did die, slowly and little by little, but I died. My own thoughts, wants, and desires fell by the wayside as you argued the life out of me.

I remember the exact moment when I gave up fighting you on our differing views of sexuality. We were sitting in a plane on the way back from China. We had been fighting about it a lot during that trip, which was not unusual for us. I remember you taking out a piece of paper and drawing a box and saying how we could live out of the box, that there was all this room out there. It was not unlike the things I'd heard you say in Florida or late in bed at night on countless, countless occasions, but something in me broke at that moment on the plane. I was so exhausted. I couldn't fight you anymore. I just couldn't. I decided then and there that I would just do it, do whatever you wanted, that I couldn't push against the current anymore, that I was tired, so tired of fighting, of conflict. I longed for peace like I've never longed for anything ever. I thought giving in to you would bring peace, but lo and behold it brought the worst chaos and torment that my soul had ever felt.

I became what you wanted and tortured myself in the process. I know you didn't mean for me to feel that way. You were also looking for your own peace, except your path to finding it was so different from my own. It was the opposite actually. Never had I seen you happier than when my soul was gagged and blindfolded, gasping for life. When I was being tortured, you were set free. A tragedy, if you ask me.

Bullet Points

- Let go.
- Don't attach to feelings as if they define me.
- Accept the moment and make peace with it as it is.
- Call myself out when I start grasping.
- Simply experience it.
- Friend and love myself.
- Hold lightly.
- Believe that I am strong enough.
- Interact with lots of people.
- Release the need to know.
- Figure out what matters to me and DO IT.
- Vocalize my feelings.
- Love with abandon.
- Make the choice to be at peace.
- Say what I want — No Fear!

Craziness

trying to describe the craziness that is my heart and brain is not the simplest of tasks.

It's a mess in there, I swear.

Emotions and thoughts collide with fears and tears. Memories of our life together.

Lately, I feel like I'm in someone else's house, cooking their food, hanging out with their friends.

My life as I've known it is gone.

Vanished . . . just like that.

Break the Cycle

i don't know when it's going to stop hurting. When will I have a week of straight happiness? I get so tired fighting for me, for what is right in my heart and mind and soul. I want to be a victim again. Someone use and abuse me, but at least I'll know my place. I won't have to struggle so much. I want peace. I want still, simple peace. No conflict. Just love and joy.

Where's my balance? Why do I lose it so easily? Why do I beg for him back after all that has transpired, after all that we went through? WE ARE NOT GOOD TOGETHER! I CAN NEVER BE TRUE TO MYSELF BY HIS SIDE! I CAN NEVER AGAIN BE HIS LOVER AND FRIEND! IT IS OVER!!!

For my sake, for my children's sake, to break this horrible cycle my family passed down generation to generation, it ends here. It ends with me. I will fight. I will conquer. I will love myself and in doing so, open myself up to loving others as unconditionally as I possibly can.

A Dream

i had a dream about you last night. You were strong and confident, yet touched my hand with tears in your eyes and said you had been wrong. You said that all you cared about was us together. You would do whatever it took. I wanted you.

I woke up, heart beating, tears in my eyes. An empty cold bed. A vague knowledge of your whereabouts. A bar, a girl, a drink. Your birthday night, out without me.

I know what my focus is right now. It is my mental wellness. I'm striving to not need anything or anyone. I will stand on my own two feet. I will establish myself and then and only then will I allow myself to want and to love another. I still hope it's you.

Our sweet daughter sits in her fort, arranged just the way she wants it. On the little table she places a picture of us four. My heart breaks a little more. I think of the love we shared and it feels unbearable. Your gentle touch, your words. I feel like death.

I feel like I want to grasp at you again, but it's the opposite of what I'm meant to do. I know it. It's okay to feel pain, I tell myself over and over and over again. It's okay.

I Want You

I let you go.
I want you.
I strive for mental and spiritual health.
I want you.
I'm establishing myself.
I want you.
I'm fucked up.
I want you.
I can exist with or without you.
I want you.
I know I drive you crazy.
I want you.
Sometimes you drive me crazy.
I want you.
I close my eyes and see you.
I open my eyes and sense you.
I want you.
I think of my blank negation.
I want you.
I think of your total drive.
I want you.

My future is a cliff.
I don't know what's beyond the drop.
I do know one thing for certain.
I want you.

Pornography

i am convinced that pornography killed my marriage. His addiction to pornography killed us. Four years of lies. Four years of cheating. Four years of wanting other women. Four years has a way of fucking with your head. And as a woman, I have a sixth sense. A knowledge of things you cannot quite explain or put your finger on, but it's there. It tells you that something is not right when a sexual woman walks by and your husband becomes tense and nervous. He would say it was me. He would blame my insecurities. I was always to blame. But the reason why I never felt wanted is simple: consciously or not, I knew that he wanted other women (the women on the screen). He wanted them and yearned for them. He was addicted to them. They filled him in ways I couldn't. I felt inadequate and undesirable.

It was a wonderful thing that he decided to confess it. Beautiful and impressive. Yet we never dealt appropriately with the fallout of his addiction. My fears and insecurities remained and then, because he wasn't looking at porn behind my back anymore, I became the crazy one. Why so much insecurity when he's not looking at it anymore? But it was too late. I had been betrayed. Sexually betrayed. One of the worst things that could have happened to me in light of my parent's drama. I view his addiction to pornography as an affair that lasted four years.

Even after it was over, it was still in his head. It had a hold on him. He had to think about other women and images from porn to become aroused. And he wanted to include me in it, maybe because he loved me so much, maybe to not feel so guilty. Whatever the reason, he needed me to be a willing participant. It didn't work if I fought him on it in the slightest because then I wasn't accepting him, I wasn't accepting his sexuality. He would label me "the brakes" and talk about how if I would just accept him, things would be different. Again, I was to blame. And there was always this pressure to be what he wanted me to be. My body became a toy, an object to use.

I just wanted to be good enough, to be able to fill him like those girls did, and so I did and said things to serve that purpose. I tried to accept him, his sexuality. I tried so hard. I would tell myself, if you can just do X then you can prove that you are no longer insecure and that you are a whole and healthy person. But that wasn't my burden to bear. Sacrifice is not a virtue, I'm learning. It was not in me to give and it was not in him to stop wanting other women. And so looking back, when all is said and done, I believe that an addiction to pornography ultimately killed my marriage.

Bits and Pieces

I stand and look down
At pieces of my heart scattered around.
Examining the pieces and trying to
　　make sense
Of what our love is or was or wasn't.
I am paralyzed as I think and remember.
I see youth hindered by fear.
I see fear, lots and lots of pieces of fear.
I see loss. I see clinging.
I see desire. Unfulfilled.
I see tears and pain and heartache.
I see you try. I see me try.
I see burdens too much to bear.
I see the word TRANSCEND.
I resent.
I resent the blame.
My fault, my fault, my fault.
The fuck it is.
I bend down. I pick up a piece. Turn it
　　over in my hand.
I pick up another and another.
I make them fit together like a puzzle.

An imperfect puzzle with holes and gaps.
I stand up with my broken heart in my
    hand.
As I walk away, I think I feel it, but I
    can't be sure.
A movement,
A pulse,
A beat.
Life.

Anger Exposed

i hate that you're a fucking whore and I hate that you ruined my life. I wish I'd never met you, never loved you, never gave you my everything. It was wasted. On a fucking whore. I hope your sexuality brings you joy, peace, and fulfillment. I hope it makes you feel secure and safe. I hope it takes care of you when you're seventy and sick. I hope it's worth it. FUCK YOU. I wish I didn't have to share a single second more of my life on or with you.

I stopped fighting because you smashed and squelched the fight right out of me. Fucking walking on egg shells around you all the time. FUCK YOU. I've loved you with everything I have and in return you tell me what a miserable sex symbol I am . . . what a useless sexual partner that only caused you pain. Well, have a great time coming on to my friend's roommate on your piece-of-shit dating website. You make me sick.

You have broken my heart into a million pieces. You have convinced yourself that what you are doing isn't wrong, that it isn't killing your soul little by little . . . that it wasn't you who broke up this family.

Hopefully you will rethink that philosophy someday, but it won't matter. It will be too late. My heart will heal. I will go on and find joy and happiness. Until then, you can kiss my ass.

Mad

You have damaged me badly. You can blame others for as long as you'd like, but in doing so you are the only one left hurting because it doesn't allow you to change yourself. I am so mad at you. I'm mad at the damage you've done to me . . . mentally, emotionally, and sexually. I'm mad that you won't allow yourself to see it and man up. Mad that I hear your voice in the back of my head all the time about how I'm wrong. Mad that you created an environment where I no longer could trust myself. Mad that you blame everything and everybody else. Mad that I'm so devastated. Mad that you squashed my dreams and stole my innocence. Mad that I still love you. Mad that you are travelling the world without me. And mad that apparently I'm following the grieving process to the letter by even being mad in the first place.

You Could . . .

the first time you see your once husband, best friend, and lover in a picture with his arm around another woman, you could feel like you want to die. You could feel like the life is being choked out of you and that there is not enough air in the room to breathe. You could run to the bathroom sobbing and in doing so you could accidentally knock over your cereal bowl and spill it all over the carpet and bed. You could cry so hard and long that you feel like you quite possibly will cry forever.

You could look at the woman staring back at you in the mirror, with red, swollen eyes and quivering lips, and feel love for the sad little girl standing there. You could take several deep, slow breaths to try to calm yourself. You could say to yourself out loud, over and over, "It's okay. It's okay. You can let him go now. Let him go."

You could realize all over again that you are not meant to be together. You could acknowledge that neither of you could give the other what they so desperately wanted and that you are better off alone or with different people. You could truly love him regardless and wish him joy and happiness. You could feel the bitter sweetness of taking another step toward emotional freedom. You could realize that you are human, give credence to those human emotions, and then speak the truth to your soul.

And the next morning you could wake up with puffy eyes and actually smile because you survived one of your biggest fears.

Innocence Lost

He yelled at me once to take down my "Happily Forever After" sign that hung above the armoire in our bedroom. It was a lie, he had shouted. Nonexistent. And that I must stop believing in it. I'm not sure who to blame for loss of innocence. I want to blame him, but I know it would have happened to me one way or another, whether he was in my life or not. Maybe I've blamed him for too much. Maybe I've blamed him for too little. I still don't know. I do know that one of my biggest fears was losing my innocence, this idea that the world was beautiful and perfect and everything I'd imagined it to be. This idea that life could imitate fairy tales. This idea of one man/one woman. This idea of bliss that doesn't end. But now I realize that life in and of itself is a vehicle for the loss of innocence. Dreams are shattered and hopes are dashed throughout the course of one's life, and the older we get, the more it happens and the truth sets in. Truth of ugliness in the world, in others, in ourselves. Truth of brokenness everywhere. Truth that in the end, we are alone.

"I keep thinking about this river somewhere, with the water moving really fast. And these two people in the water, trying to hold onto each other, holding on as hard as they can, but in the end it's just too much. The current's too strong. They've got to let go, drift apart. That's how I think it is with us. It's a shame because we've loved each other all our lives. But in the end, we can't stay together forever."

Kazuo Ishiguro, *Never Let Me Go*

A Letter to My Love

Hi love,

It's sure been a while. For all this time I've been trying to put the pieces together, trying to figure out the equation, trying to distribute blame. I'm on the cusp of completing the picture, the puzzle.

And I realize there is no blame to place, no fingers to point. It comes down to two human beings doing the very best they knew how with the examples and resources they were given as they grew up. The voids in me, I looked for you to fill, and the voids in you, you looked for me to fill.

My main desire was to feel validated and worthy. My whole self hinged on whether you found me good enough. But that's not how it works. And I became a shell of a human being. In the end, I can't blame you for anything because I am responsible for myself and my actions. And I was weak and immature and controlled by fear. It became a mess. A mess of emotions, thoughts, conflicts.

But despite it all, there has always been love. The difference is that the love I have now is not desperate or grasping. My love for you is free. I send it to you with no strings attached and no obligations and no fear. It just is. This love longs for the best for you, even as it doesn't involve me.

I cry as I write this, because I can't believe how far I've come. I've always wanted to give you this kind of love, but the brokenness inside of me wouldn't allow it. I am becoming whole and the more whole I become, the more true love I can give out. As part of that, I want you to live your best life; to find deep joy and happiness, to find more love, to be your highest and best self. You are amazing and I love you.

Baggage

The bag of shit is gone now.
Falling, falling down
Along with you.
I had to drop all of it.
I had to drop all of those I've ever
     cared about.
I had to free myself from people
To find myself.

Proof of My Love

i used to think that giving you my soul was the greatest proof of my love to you. I was mistaken. Owning my soul is the highest and greatest proof of my love.

This Thing

This thing, whatever it is, has a mind
of its own.
I try to control and restrain it, but it
speeds off, happy and passionate.
It heads somewhere, it has a
destination in mind.
Yet it doesn't share it with me. It can't.
It won't.
My only choice is to follow.
Yet in the back of my head:
The fears
The lack
The insecurity
The craziness
The issues
They are still there.

Guarding My Heart

Why do I give my heart so easily?
Not just to anybody, but when I feel
    it, I give it.
All of it.
I can't hold back.
I don't know how to give just a piece.
I must guard it, very carefully.
I must watch it.
How quickly it runs off . . .
How desperately it longs to love and
    be loved.

Where I Belong

An interaction.
Trepidatious.
A tiptoe.
A glance.
A gentle push
And then hold my breath.
Sweet words,
Beautiful and strong.
Truth spoken.
Nothing more pure.
Logic versus emotion.
I want you.
I'll wait.
I need you.
Not really.
I want to need you.
Yes, that's it.
Power in desire, so fierce.
And I let go again.
Release hope and expectations.
Release fears and panic.
Settle into peace.
This is where I belong.

The Wait

What is this void I'm trying to fill?
Why do I ache and panic?
It's love.
I want to be loved,
Purely
Beautifully
Perfectly
Unconditionally.
I believe if I can give such love, surely
    one day I will receive it back.
Someday it will come out of nowhere
    and put my whole world on its side.
Someday it will find me,
Right?
Isn't that what happens?
How the story goes?
Or maybe, just maybe, I can love myself
    enough
That I am not desperate for that love
    from someone else.
Is it possible? Feasible? Likely?
I don't know, but until then,
I wait.

The Hunt for Love

i just finished writing my third speech for Toast-masters. It's about inauthenticity and the destruction it leaves behind. I was inauthentic for a good part of my life. Being who everyone else wanted me to be in order to feel love, acceptance, and validation. Amazingly, I've found a new way to live. All these things I was searching for in other people, have been inside of me all along. Do I like other people's love, acceptance, and validation? Hell yes I do. But I don't NEED it. I am not dependent on it, which allows me to be who I truly am, in all circumstances. And I love it.

Don Miguel Ruiz says it beautifully:

"The love we need to hunt is inside ourselves, but that love is difficult prey. . . . If you can capture the prey, you will see that your love can grow strong inside you, and it can fulfill your needs. This is so important for your happiness."

From *The Mastery of Love*

My First Love

i want to tell you about my first love.

He was handsome, this first love of mine, and when he held my hand I was the happiest girl in the world. He was funny and charismatic, always engaging with people, wanting to know their story. He laughed good and he laughed hard. He would sing show tunes at the top of his lungs and grab me and swing me around the room dancing. He made me happy. He would plan dates for us to go on, the most memorable one being a Broadway show in New York City. He made me feel special. He was my hero and my friend. My first love was my dad.

When I was sixteen years old, my parents sat my brother and me down at our local Carl's Jr. and told us that my dad "struggled with homosexuality." They could have just as well told me that my friend was a Martian or that my dog was a crocodile. It just did not compute. My parents were missionaries, for crying out loud, spreading the good news and living according to biblical standards. None of it made any sense, and it all made me feel sick to my stomach. Who was this man sitting across from me eating his Famous Star with cheese? Who was he . . . really? This was my first encounter with deep-rooted dishonesty or, better said, inauthenticity. Something being completely different than what it was portrayed to be.

That night I went to bed and cried and cried and cried. After all the crying, I decided that I was in too much pain, that I couldn't bear to feel this weight and this amount of sadness and confusion, and so I took that information and stuffed it in a file and hid that file way back in the archives of my brain. If I couldn't deal with it, I would just act as though it didn't exist. That was the beginning of my life being lived in denial. It was easier to ignore, easier to turn a blind eye, than to really feel that hurt and pain and betrayal.

Now, looking back, I realize that at some point in my own life, I began living my own type of inauthentic life. I began believing that if I was to be loved and accepted, I had to be what everyone expected me to be. I couldn't question. I couldn't rock the boat. I couldn't Just. Be. Me.

And so I stepped into a role of making everyone else happy and in that process became hugely codependent. I did everything for everyone else (especially in my marriage), but at the end of the day, it was selfish. I didn't do it for them or him. I did it for me, to feel loved, appreciated, valued. It was a way to control and to manipulate others to get what I wanted, what I longed for. Their love and acceptance, their approval and validation, happened to be my drugs of choice. At the end of the day my inauthenticity destroyed everything in its path.

Destruction, devastation, annihilation, and trash is what inauthenticity leaves behind. I don't beat myself up about the inauthenticity in my life. I recognize that it was a process I had to go through and it was a pattern I had to break. As a young girl, I was given a daily example of inauthenticity. The person I most loved was a counterfeit, a fake, not the real deal. And as children we soak up all that we are exposed to, and many times it becomes a part of us as well. That is, unless we decide that we've had enough and that the patterns and traits we picked up are not serving us any longer.

I feel at peace now because through this journey I have discovered a love inside myself that is greater than anything I can possibly find on the outside, and that love has allowed me to release this addiction to people's approval. I hope my son and daughter remember a mom whose thoughts, actions, and character were all congruent, a mom who was content with herself and therefore had no need to get affirmation elsewhere, a mom who practiced what she preached and was real and genuine. As a matter of fact, I think I'm going to read some Dr. Seuss to my kids tonight. And it will go something like this . . .

"Be who you are and say what you say, because those who mind don't matter and those who matter don't mind."

A speech given at Toastmasters.

Broken

Something inside
Something is off
Not right
Broken
Bleeding
Unsure
Scared
Deep down
I wrestle with it
Struggle and fight
Against it
Sometimes something
Clicks
And I feel whole.
But only for a moment
Because I'm broken.
How and when can I fix this
Broken part of me?

Living Proof

Wish I was feeling better,
    but some days you just don't.
Wish the tears would stop,
    but sometimes they just won't.
Wish I was completely healed,
    but some journeys take time.
Wish I could just jump ahead,
    and leave this pain behind.
My heart is tarred and closed
    and prickly to the touch
But someday after all the pain,
    it will open oh so much.
The process can be a bitch,
    of crazy ups and downs,
Of digging deep, of cutting in,
    of sobs and other sounds.
But I am not discouraged,
    I will keep my head up high
For after all the cutting,
    I know the blood will dry.
And I have to share it all,
    otherwise I will be stuck

Back in that place of misery where
    I don't give a fuck.
Part of the process is letting go of
    what you think of me.
So am I sorry that I just cussed?
    I'm not . . . I'll let it be.
The path to self-discovery is lonely,
    yes indeed,
But through it I believe I'll find the
    people that I need.
What am I to lose if I put it all out
    on the line?
My ego may be bruised a bit,
    but at this point that's fine.
Nothing to lose right now
    but my being and my truth.
And those two things mean every-
    thing. We are all living proof.

Speak My Truth

i remember the meeting all too well. It is etched in my mind's eye. I feel the heat in the air, see the bodies in the room. This was a family meeting, and a very serious one at that. I am sitting next to my dad. He is tense and I can feel his nervous vibe. My mom has eleven brothers and sisters, and they are mostly all there with their spouses telling my mom why they disagree with her decision to remarry my dad.

"He hasn't changed."

"He's not repentant."

"He will only hurt you again."

"We will not support this wedding."

The air is thick with disdain and resentment. One of my aunts pulls out a dictionary and starts reading the definition for pedophile.

You see, my dad sexually molested my mom's younger brother, my uncle, when they were away on a missions trip. My dad was not only his family at this point, but his leader as well. My uncle was fifteen when the abuse occurred. This has been something that I've been so ashamed of from the moment I learned about it ten years ago until this very moment. It's something that I can't quite wrap my mind around, much less know what to do about it, and for whatever reason, I feel responsible somehow. In a way, I took on the guilt and shame of my dad's actions. Not only that, but I feel like my talking about this family secret makes me a rat somehow, like I am betraying my family. My dad. My uncle. Everyone. But recently I've been having this constant nagging push to "Speak my truth."

It's funny that the objective of this speech is to use body language appropriately because everything about what I'm sharing makes my body tense up, my heart pound in my chest, and my legs begin to shake. I've been wrestling with whether to talk about this or not. It's something that I haven't even shared with many of my close friends, but I keep hearing this internal voice, this prodding, telling me to "Speak my truth." I need to talk about the facts of my life from beginning to end because secrecy and shame will rot my bones and poison my soul. They already have.

Why do I need to speak my truth? Why do I think it is important for all of us to speak our truth? I believe that the truth will set me free. I believe that by speaking our truths, we will be set free from the prisons we lock ourselves in. Prisons of fear and shame, behind bars of guilt and doubt. Prisons of isolation, believing no one else could ever understand. I believe that is an illusion because we are all one. In some ways, my truth is your truth and your truth is mine, in the emotions we feel, in our base needs and wants. We are all one. So when one of us speaks our truth, it gives the rest of us permission to do the same.

Speaking our truth is us acknowledging that This Thing happened in our lives. It gives us the opportunity to truly grieve and then to do the miraculous; let it go. We cannot let go of something we haven't even acknowledged as happening. I'm not suggesting that everyone go out and scream it from the mountaintops, but in some fashion the truth needs to be spoken. Speak it to a counselor, to a good friend, to a stranger. It doesn't matter, so long as your truth is spoken. People in this room have spoken their truth in front of us, and it's memorable and impactful and we can all relate on some level. It unites us and our love begins to grow. Intimacy grows. A feeling of oneness emerges.

My family issues are far from resolved. My parents remarried. None of my mom's siblings went to the wedding. Life is messy and complicated, but at the end of the day all I am responsible for is myself. My heart. My life. My choices. And I choose to face these issues head on. I will no longer live in denial. I will no longer block out events because they cause me pain. I will look at them and I will talk about them because I truly believe that is the key to my healing and maybe to the healing of others as well. And the pain that I feel is a different kind of pain. It's productive pain. It hurts like hell, but I can tell it is doing something, it's getting me somewhere, as opposed to the pain you feel when you're just stuck. It's pain with a purpose.

I am done only looking for comfort. I want to live FULLY. I am committed to living each moment completely engaged, beautiful or painful as the moment may be.

A speech given for Toastmasters.

Family Secrets

Deep dark family secrets.

What to do with the knowledge, with the
information, with the facts, with the
emotions.

How much to say? How much to share? How
to express it?

I am NOT responsible. But I FEEL responsible.

For you. For your actions. For your lies and
your abuse.

And for her. I feel responsible for her.

For her secret keeping and betrayal.

Too many secrets. Too many lies. Too many
people to protect.

But I am urged to expose. To uncover. To
bring to the light.

Your sins.

There Are Days to Feel Sad

There are days to feel sad.
Days when the heart is heavy and sunken in.
Days when it feels hard to breathe
And the tears are always there covering the eyes.
Days when little things feel like a struggle
And big things feel like an impossibility.
I used to try to fight those days,
To ignore them and pretend they didn't exist.
Now I just sit here and feel the sadness,
Feel my sunken-in and heavy heart,
Allow the tears to fall down my face,
And feel all the hurt and the pain and the grief.
I accept that I am feeling the way I am,
and then, a miraculous thing happens.
This acceptance of my pain sets me free.
Not immediately, not right away . . .
But inevitably, it always sets me free.
Free to once again dust off my wings
And fly.

The Present

Come back, I call out to myself.
Come back to the present.
The fields are open and spacious out here.
The air, breathe it in, it's clean and it's pure.
Come back from the past with its pain
    and its guilt.
Come back from the future with its
    hopes and its fears.
Come back to this moment where truth
    and love lie.
Return to it and rest reassured.
All that I have is this second in time.
Embrace it and love it and linger and stay.
On this very moment of this very day.

A Solitary Holiday

What do I have to be thankful for on this Thanksgiving Day as I sit alone in my house?

I want to feel sorry for myself, to sink down into a deep depression, to tell myself how lame I must be to be without husband or kids or family on this special day. I want to, but I won't. I will concentrate on the peace I feel inside. I will focus on the peace of loving myself and respecting my boundaries. I will smile at the dog curled up in my lap and feel the heat from the fire. I will laugh occasionally at the silly Thanksgiving commercials on TV and root for the underdogs in the NFL. I will be happy that I am who I am and accept the place I'm at in life. I will wish the best for others this day as they celebrate their families and loved ones. I will be happy for them. But one thing I know for certain. I will never take another people-filled, chaotic, fun, and exhausting Thanksgiving for granted again.

I Want, I Need, I Desire

I want freedom.
I need love.
I desire life.
I want love.
I need affection.
I desire intimacy.
I want a man.
I need kisses.
I desire to orgasm.
I want love.
I need care.
I desire purpose.
I want fun.
I need security.
I desire options.
I want peace.
I need less strife.
I desire fulfillment.
I want to know what I stand for.
I need to belong.
I desire happiness.

I want solitude.
I need friends.
I desire the combination.
I want life.
I need strength.
I desire to be great.
I want to be known.
I need love.
I desire respect.
I want approval.
I need self-approval.
I desire to be true to myself.
I want to laugh with someone.
I need good sex.
I desire to feel good about sex.

My Highest Hope

Getting to know a man,
Realizing he just might be
What I need.
Something feels
So right.
I want to take it slow
And I do.
Yet I long for more,
Just a little more
Of his love and his life.
I feel that with him
I can do it.
Love him without losing
Me.
And love me without losing
Him.
That is my highest hope.

A Self-Fulfilling Prophecy

i did it. I destroyed it all. I keep destroying it all. Over and over and over again. Destruction.

No trust. Lack of trust. I will never trust again. I don't know how. It's broken. SHATTERED. And now all I know to do is repel people. First attract then repel, but not without first causing myself immense amounts of pain.

A self-fulfilling prophecy, is what he said. Yes, I keep fulfilling my own prophecy.

My First Hypnotherapy Session

"Close your eyes and relax. Take a deep breath and feel the chair under your body. I want you to think about why you're here today. Think about what you want to get out of this session. What do you see?" she asks.

"I see a girl, confident, dark hair, and wind blowing her hair around gently, standing tall."

"What is the girl telling you?"

"She says, 'Just Be.'"

My hypnotherapist tells me to walk down the five steps before me into my safe place. She guides me step-by-step, and when I'm at the last step, she asks me what I see.

"Dark," I reply.

"What do you feel?"

"Fear," and I start to cry.

She tells me that I'm doing a good job, to let it go. She tells me to envision a clear bubble in front of me and to put the fear and darkness in that bubble. I imagine it. She tells me to watch it disappear into the universe.

"The universe will take care of your fear now," she says. And then, "Now what do you see in your safe place?"

"It's empty."

"Good, do you want to create your safe place right now?"

"Yes," I whisper.

"Okay. What do you see in your safe place?"

"A rainbow."

"Anything else?"

"Birds and a tree."

"What is the floor like that you're standing on?"

"It's white."

"Good. What else do you see?"

"A girl."

"Is it the same girl you saw at the beginning?"

"Yes."

"I want you to face that girl. What do you see or feel?"

I start to cry again. "Confidence," I say. "And peace."

"Good. Now I want you to feel the vibrations of this confident feeling. Where do you feel it in your body?"

"In my core."

"I want you to allow that vibration of confidence to travel throughout your body," she instructs me.

My body feels warm, hot almost.

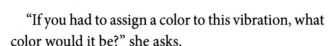

"If you had to assign a color to this vibration, what color would it be?" she asks.

"Blue."

"Okay, whenever you see the color blue you will think about this vibration and feeling of confidence."

"Okay," I say

"Now what else do you see in your safe place?"

"The floor has changed. I'm outside now, with the rainbow, the birds, a tree, butterflies. There is a blanket laid out on the grass. And the girl is watching me from a distance," I explain.

"What are you feeling?"

"I am happy, but I want a man."

"It's time to leave your safe place. Walk slowly back up the stairs. Five, four, three, two, one. Now open your eyes."

A Journey Inward

A heaviness, a weight, a burden
Loss of breath, tightness in my chest
A panic rising.
I recognize this feeling.
I despise this feeling.
Attachment, loss of control, fear,
The feelings engulf me.
I'm drowning
In a big dark sea
Of loneliness and despair.
Wanting to be loved purely, convincingly,
No pull back, no doubts.
Not convinced that it's humanly possible.
But still holding out, still believing
In fairy tales.

Hi, my name is Janice Angela Burt and I wrote this poem on May 23rd, 2012. Now I want to read you another poem that I wrote just four months later:

You act like a new convert, he said.
The energy, the passion, the excitement.
Yes! I am a new convert.
Converted from death to life,
From hopelessness to unending
    possibilities.
Converted from fear to love,
From the bitterness of despair to the
    lightness of joy.
Converted from denial to awareness,
From the darkness of my self-made prison
    to the wide expanse of my safe place.
I am truly a new person, unrecognizable
    at times to myself anymore.
I never knew I could be so free, so driven,
    so undeniably ME!

What made the difference? From the first heavy, dark, depressing poem that I wrote, to the second light, joyful, exuberant poem? The difference was a journey inward, a journey to my soul, a peek at the essence of my being, an encounter with my ideal self.

I lay there, relaxed. My body feels as if it's one with the chair. I hear her voice, calm and soothing, guiding me to a peaceful state. She tells me to envision a staircase and to go down the stairs and into my safe place. I freeze. You see, my safe place is black, dark as night, and I'm scared. I can't go in. She asks me what I see and then asks me what I feel. "Fear" is all I manage to say, and tears stream down my face. It's too scary to go in there. I don't feel like I can do it. She tells me to visualize a bubble and to put all the blackness and all the fear into that bubble and to watch it float away. "You don't need that anymore," she says. "You can let it go."

This was how my first hypnotherapy session started. I've done counseling before. I've been involved in marriage groups before (I've taken them and taught them). When my ex-husband and I were trying to make our marriage work, we saw a therapist every week for a while. While counseling is good, none of it ever had the effect on me that this one hypnotherapy session did. It was life-changing. And I believe that the difference was that I went inward. I met myself for the first time, so to speak.

It seems to me that we have our conscious mind that talks and talks and reasons and justifies and blames and thinks and thinks, but the problem is that lots of these thoughts are the thoughts that we've been conditioned to think, thoughts that other people told us to think, and beliefs that others told us to believe. But beyond that, deep inside of each of us, there lies the most beautiful thing of all . . . our soul, our being, us truly. Unfortunately, it gets covered up by fears, layer upon layer of fear. And before we know it, we are locked in a prison. We look down and see the key dangling out of our pocket. But, although it's a prison, it's our safe prison, and so we stay and we eat hard bread and wear a forced smile on our lips.

That was me, just a year ago. I was locked up. I had so many fears: fear of not being good enough, fear of rejection, fear of loss, fear of not being loved, fear of not mattering to anyone, especially not myself, fear of change, and fear of the unknown.

And then I journeyed inward and not only created my safe place but also saw my ideal self. She was this confident, peaceful, strong woman! So I decided that I was ready to free the starving prisoner girl in order that she might become this other woman. One that I always thought was in me, but one that I could never quite become. Until now. I realized that all the love I needed was hidden inside ME! My eyes were opened to the fact that I no longer needed to get other people's validation and thumbs-up to be an okay human being.

I was enough.

I will always be enough.

A speech given at Toastmasters.

Bring the Love Back

The journey's so hard, the trek is quite long,
But the beauty that's me has been there all along.
There is no comparing, no competition, no game.
I am so unique and you are just the same.
The love that I feel growing in me is deep.
Not sure how it got there, perhaps you find what
    you seek.
My ego fills up on accolades and praise.
My ego's a trap, a diversion, a maze.
But my intuition, I feel, is true every time.
It is loving and strong and guides me just fine.
I love that my life is a movie indeed,
With scenes to be written and scripts we can
    read.
And your life is, too, and some parts overlap.
We can all help each other to bring the Love back.

Just Be

The struggle.
The incessant struggle of it all.
I'm tired, worn to the bone.
Pushing and striving.
I think it's time for me to just be.
My ideal self told me to "Just Be."
Just be tired.
Just be overwhelmed.
Just be upset.
Just be sad.
Just Be.
Why is it so hard for me to just be?

Dear Pastor

Hi! This is a bit random for me. I have never sent an email to a pastor before, but I just had to write one to you. I don't know how much background to give. I'm sure you are swamped with church duties, family life, and community events just to name a few, so I don't want to take up a lot of your time. Suffice it to say that I was a missionary kid in Mexico City for five years, grew up in the church, discovered my dad was gay, went through a nasty church split involving my father-in-law, had my husband turn into an adamant atheist, compromised myself to continue that relationship for a number of years, decided I had to get a divorce, and am in the final stages of that process at this very moment. I have two beautiful children.

When my husband decided to become an atheist, I didn't know what to do. He was my leader for all the years we'd been married. I clung to him fiercely. I didn't know how to make my own decisions. As he pulled away from God and all the things we'd been taught concerning Jesus and the Bible, I began to do the same. I didn't have a true, personal relationship with God. I borrowed everyone else's relationship with Him. I was a people pleaser and just did what I thought everyone wanted me to do. I had been surrounded by so much judgment, so many rules, so much condemnation. No one seemed genuine, everyone felt fake to me. But I didn't want to let them down. I didn't want to be judged (I believe that this partially comes from the excommunication of my dad in front of the entire congregation some years back).

All that being said, when I began to feel a tugging on my heart to go to a church, I was very reluctant. Very, very reluctant. I decided to go anyway. The first Sunday I went, you spoke about the difference between the Spirit and the Letter of the Law. I knew exactly what you were talking about, the people that walk around with these spiritually beautiful robes on, but death inside. They are all dressed up in religion. Then just this past Sunday, you spoke about our attitudes being open to what God has for us. And that when we're in a relationship with Him, we WANT to improve our lives. We no longer feel that we HAVE to. I am experiencing that very thing right now. I had always felt that I HAD to follow certain rules yet that was incarceration for me, but now I feel like I WANT to do other things: godlier, healthier, eternal things. The difference between doing something because you "want" to versus because you feel you "have" to is remarkable.

I think I'm rambling now. I hope some of that made sense. You are so right on the target with what you teach. Your sermon from last Sunday was so well put and perfectly worded. You said that God had made you understand it and you'd hoped that some of us would too, and I just want you to know that I understood and agree and was encouraged in this tough spot I find myself in life right now. So thank you.

Janice Burt

Peace from God?

Where does this peace I'm feeling come from?
Is it God?
I know that's the "right" answer, but is it the
    "true" answer?
Something deep down says yes, but other
    voices interfere.
The voice of skepticism . . . saying I'm a fool.
The voice of bitterness . . . saying I've had
    enough.
The voice of experience . . . saying that path's
    no good.
The voice of anger . . . saying I'll just be judged.
Despite these voices, there remains this inner
    peace that I can't deny.
It's like a guiding force that makes my steps
    sure and stable.
It gives me confidence and a calm spirit.
This connection that I speak of is mine alone.
I don't want to share it with anyone, lest they
    taint it
With their views, and thoughts, and opinions.

I don't want anyone else's words to disrupt my
     hope.
I want to keep it hidden till I figure out what I
     must do with it.
I consider it a mysterious treasure.
How else can one walk so peaceful through a
     tornado
Or sleep so sound through a landslide?
Peace from God, yes, perhaps.
This has yet to be decided.

Divinity Within

How to talk about this Divinity inside me?
How to describe something so
    mysteriously amazing?
Mere words do nothing to explain this
    part of my life, of who I am.
How can words describe something so
    magnificent,
So life-giving, so whole and peaceful?
There is no need to talk about it, I suppose.
To convince, to explain, or to defend.
It just is. And talking about it or not, does
    not change what is.
That this Divinity exists deep inside of me.
All the words from my past repulse me.
And the words from my present don't do
    it justice.
So I just sit here with this beautiful
    knowledge that cannot be shared,
But must only be experienced.
And still, after going over words in my
    head, I come back only to one:
LOVE.

Uncovering Love

this life is a journey, a quest. We are searching. We are seeking. Constantly searching and seeking for something to fill this gap, this space in our souls.

U2 still hasn't found what they're looking for. And The Rolling Stones can't get no satisfaction. No matter how great or talented or how much money we make, we are on a quest, each one of us, to fill the empty space.

We look high and we look low. We try things on for size. We live and we learn. We fall and we get back up. I think I've found what my soul longs for . . . Love. Not an outside love that will disappoint and upset, but a Love that comes from within myself. A Love that comes from an empowered heart. A Love that is in all of us, but gets buried over time, trapped under fears and doubts and shame and guilt.

My quest and my journey in life is to uncover this Love. What an adventure!

Fear versus Love

So much discord all around me. So many people fastened to their points of view. So much ego to wade through. And I, do I want to be part of the problem? Or is there a better way, another path?

Love, to me, means acceptance, pure and total acceptance of the BEING, not necessarily of the DOING. Love is seeing beyond the ugly, past the broken, over the heap of trash. It doesn't mean the ugly, broken trash is not there. It just means we have vision that goes deeper, eyes that see through, and compassion that "gets it."

It's easy to say, until the action of another hits us right between the eyes and sets off all our triggers. Then it comes down to Fear versus Love. Which one will I choose today?

I Cried

after hearing the news yesterday, I sat down and cried.

I cried for lost lives and for lost innocence.

I cried for broken hearts and shattered dreams.

I cried for humanity. I cried for the lack of love.

And then I dried my eyes and sat down and thought.

I thought about my own kid's lives, their hopes and dreams.

I thought about my interaction with them day to day.

I thought about how I don't know what tomorrow may bring into their lives, and how I can't control it all.

After thinking for quite a while, I sat down and reassessed my priorities.

I decided to do my very, very best to be truly present with them when they are with me.

I determined to put down my phone so that I can hear about the little funny details about their day at school . . . or the boy Ella chases . . . or the video game Samuel can't stop talking about.

I decided to live every second with them as if it were their last, because there are no guarantees that they will be around tomorrow. The safety nets that I put in place are all just illusions.

So, with that in mind, I am committed to live even deeper and more present than I am doing today.

I am committed to pursuing a life of love, a life of passion, and a life of meaning.

And I will do this whether I have one day or seventy years left on this planet.

The world can change, one heart at a time.

Thoughts after the elementary school massacre in Connecticut.

The Choice

Wow, so many thoughts after each tragedy. We are all one. I am the bomber. I am the saint. I am the child. I am the rapist. I am the darkness. I am the light. I am capable of it all. The victim and the perpetrator. The gossip that tears down and the kind word that inspires. The selfish prick who laughs and mocks the unfortunate and the kind-hearted soul who spends her time in their service. I am capable of it all.

What lies before me then is a choice. A path to choose, and it starts and stops in my mind, in the deep dark recesses of my brain, my thoughts. Where to go from here? Every second of every day, we have a choice.

There is a bumpy path, with dips and divots; the ground is uneven and rough, but the sun is always shining and there is peace in the air. That path is love. There is a smoother path, that initially looks easier, but you go down that path a little ways and there is a steep drop-off into darkness and other unimaginable terrors. That path is fear.

I am capable of love as much as I am capable of fear. Choose. Choose we must. Every second of every day.

Thoughts after the Boston Marathon bombing.

Where Are the Men?

MEN! Where are the men?
Stand up. Please stand up. We need you.
We need your strength, we need your
goodness.
We long for your purity, for your
protection.
We need strong, powerful, loving men
Who lift up and do not destroy,
Who rescue and do not steal youth and
innocence.
Men who don't abuse and abandon.
Men who care.
Why are you looking at the guy next to
you?
It starts with you, only with you.
We will know who you are by your
actions,
Regardless of the words you speak.
We will be in awe of your integrity,
A blinding light to all who see it.
And it will change the world.

Men, please, please stand up.
I beg this of you.

*Written after hearing about the kidnapping
and abuse endured by three women in Ohio.*

Letter to Oprah

Question on Oprah.com: *Has positive thinking changed your life? If yes, how so?*

Wow! And yes! Positive thinking has indeed changed my life.

Brief background: I was raised in a fundamentalist Christian home and spent five years in Mexico City as an MK (missionary kid). As a teenager, I found out that my dad was gay, and that knowledge turned my world upside down. I didn't know how to process the information and so I began living in denial. If something hurt, I hightailed it out of there mentally. I lived like an ostrich (with my head stuck in the sand). I married my childhood sweetheart when I was twenty. For the next fourteen years of marriage, I lost myself more and more and more, until I didn't know who I was anymore. I felt my intuition whisper things to me, but I was an expert at ignoring her and only caring about what others thought of me and how others viewed me. I felt that if I could have their love and approval, I would be worth something and have value.

My husband became an atheist about nine years into our marriage. This also turned my world upside down because I could no longer just follow in his shadow. I had to make a decision. I chose to follow him, believing that he was all I had and his acceptance of me was of utmost importance. The problem was that his view of sexuality is very different than mine at a core level, and it had always been a problem for us. He would push me to do more and more "out of the box" sexual activities. And again, my intuition would scream NO but my need for acceptance was so high that I would give in time and time again. In the end, it was too much. After two years of living like this, totally contrary to what I wanted and who I was, I told him I wanted a separation. The pain had become more than I could bear and being without him seemed, although equally torturous, a better path. I have been divorced for seven months now.

In the past year and a half I have completely changed my way of thinking. I used to think that I needed other people's validation and their OK to feel secure in myself and to feel that I was enough. Now, I get that validation from within, from that place deep inside (the true me) that for so long I neglected and abused. I even went so far as to dedicate a love song to myself: "The Reason" by Hoobastank.

I now know I am enough, with or without another person's validation and approval. Changing my thought patterns did take time. It took me a good solid year to replace my negative perspectives with positive ones. And in all reality, I feel that really it is just a lifelong process. I read lots of self-help books, I meditated, I saw a therapist, and then I saw a hypnotherapist. Immediately after seeing the hypnotherapist, I felt that the pieces of the puzzle started coming together for me. I felt whole. I discovered my subconscious. I saw my fear and I was able to release it. I also saw my ideal self and was able to actually become her. Better said, I was able to become the me I had so neglected out of fear. I have learned to look my fears straight in the eye and push through them, walk through them. I have learned to sit with the pain and not run from it. I would cry for hours and hours and have panic attacks often, especially at night, but as horrible as it was, I would wake up the next day and realize that I actually made it through and I didn't die. Little by little, I became stronger.

I view everything differently now. I do my best not to take things personally anymore. I don't compare myself to others like I used to. I realize now that we are each on our own path, so when I start to compare myself with others I quickly turn my eyes inward and focus instead on bettering myself.

I joined the Runnin' for Rhett training team and am practicing to run my first half and full marathons this year. I used to have such a victim mentality: Why is all of this happening to me? Now, I am proactive and go for what I want. I also stay away from those things that I don't want.

I recently became state-certified as a Spanish court interpreter and am just now getting into the voice-over industry. I am passionate about connecting with people. I feel this strange connection to humanity now. I have had to learn to sacrifice short-term pleasure for my long-term wants. This is mainly regarding romantic relationships. I feel lonely sometimes and so I think I want a man right now, but in all reality, I know I need to continue working on myself so that I don't get into a relationship and have the same type of problems that I did in my last one. So I figure that it's okay to be lonely now because my HIGHEST want is a healthy relationship in the future.

I am living my dream life right now, in this very second. I am aware, I am positive, I am me . . . fully ME. And nothing could be better than that!

Past Lives

i purchased a Groupon for a past-life regression group hypnotherapy session. I had no idea what to expect, but it looked interesting. I thought the session was going to deal with my past life as in when I was a child and in my younger years.

It was only after I was sitting in a room full of people and the hypnotherapist was explaining it all, that I realized that past-life regression was based on the belief system of reincarnation and we were actually going to go take a peek into our own past lives. Whaaat? Now, I am and was then in the process of figuring out for myself what my own belief systems are, discarding some that I only had because I grew up with them and adopting others that I sensed are right based on my own gut feelings toward them. But this, this was way outside of the box.

It's okay, I thought. I knew that I was right where I needed to be, and if something felt wrong or contrary to ME, I would just walk out. I decided that, regardless of whether or not I believe in reincarnation, I could get something out of this exercise. I also decided to be open and let my inner being take me where it wanted me to go.

There were about twenty of us in the room. I was lying on the ground. The hypnotherapist told us to relax and get comfortable. She told us that we were going to go back into several different lives that we've lived. I closed my eyes and focused on her voice and drifted inside of myself.

In a hallway there is a door with light shining from under it. I open the door and I go in. There are five doors in a circle all around me. I open the door immediately to my left and into my first life experience. All I see is a baby.

I go to the second door. The hypnotherapist tells us that we are going back 100 to 200 years ago. I open that door and all I see is darkness.

Next is the third door. We are going back 500 to 800 years ago. I see a woman in a stiff dress, long sleeves, embroidered, going all the way up and around the neck. She reminds me of an old-time queen, like out of Alice in Wonderland. She just stands there, looking at me, and that is all I see.

I go to the fourth door. This, she says, is our most happy past life. There I am at a wooden kitchen table, pots on the stove, food being cooked. I'm sitting down surrounded by children. I am holding a toddler in my arms and I'm laughing. The baby is laughing. Everyone is warm and safe. It's like out of *Little House on the Prairie* and I am filled with the most peaceful sensation.

Now I am at the fifth and last door; this is my most important past life. I am in a harem. There are several women there, not necessarily happy, but not unhappy either. We are there just being used for sex. My hands are handcuffed above my head. I'm naked. There is just one man there. I don't recognize the man. He goes around taking time on each woman. I see my feet, I feel my nakedness. Later in that same life, I'm in a hallway, passionately kissing that same man. There is something special between us. Love? Passion at least. I feel a strong connection. Then, I'm having this man's baby, but he is not there by my side. And later still, I'm lying in a bed holding my baby and I die peacefully. My soul leaves my body.

As we finish looking at our past lives, the hypno-therapist tells us to envision climbing up a staircase. She asks us why we believe that we are here in this present life. What mission do we need to complete? What challenges do we need to finally overcome? As I look into myself for the answers, I sense that I am here to be empowered, to take my power back. I was so powerless in my past life. I was used. I am here to develop and project my own voice.

As I walk up the stairs that I was told to envision, I see my beautiful authentic self in her white flowing dress, and she gives me a gift. I open the box to find a glowing bright-red heart inside. I put it up to my own physical heart and my body accepts it. In that instant, I feel unconditional love. I feel it for humanity, for those who have knowingly or unknowingly hurt me, for myself. This love shines through my entire being.

And then the session is over and I walk out the door, into the world. However, the world is a little different than it was an hour before. My perception has shifted.

Transformation

How many lives do we live in this one single life we are given?

Our lives change so slowly, almost imperceptibly until we wake up one morning and we realize very acutely that we are not the same person who fell asleep last night. We have become another. Our thoughts and perceptions have evolved. Experiences have left their mark. Time has bent and shaped us. We lie there and feel like a stranger to ourselves, like a parasite invading another being.

It is an uncomfortable yet strangely calming feeling. It is as though I knew I was meant to be here all along, one day. Almost like the transformation of a caterpillar into its flying state. The wings are useful, but the butterfly doesn't quite know what to do with them yet. I've woken up today in another life, another mind, another heart. Now if I could just figure out how to fly . . .

Reiki

i did my first Reiki session today. Before a week ago, I hadn't even heard of Reiki. It's amazing all the different things I learn about and neat people I meet through these networking meetings.

She had me lie on a massage table and close my eyes. She scanned my head with her hands and said there was a lot of activity going on, lots of thoughts zooming around. Then, as her hands moved to my neck, she said it was like I was choking. It was like I was trying to get words out, but they were stuck in my throat. There was a disconnect between my head and my heart, she told me. There was some blockage. The passage from my head to my heart was blocked.

She felt anger. She felt lots of anger in me. She saw, in my heart, a rose. It was a tight bud of a rose that had a tarlike substance on it. She said that I had to get the tar off and then the rose would bloom. She told me that I had a lot in my subconscious mind and that it would be a good idea to go back and revisit that to be able to clear it out.

She moved down and scanned my right hand, and saw a pen in it and saw me writing. She explained that she felt that writing would be a big part of my life, bigger than maybe I even thought it would be. In my other hand, she saw a microphone. She saw me speaking and felt that I had something to share and that when I was able to unblock the passage from my head to my heart, the words would pour out seamlessly.

She said that I would know when the right man came along. I would know and not to worry about that, but for now to really think and write down what I want in a man and in a relationship. She told me to be very specific in the traits and qualities that I was looking for. She suggested I do a ritual of sorts to let my ex-husband go, for she saw great potential in me once my heart is free.

She then saw me, my authentic self, standing tall and looking out over a cliff to the ocean. I was peaceful and powerful. I was secure and confident. I had found my voice, at last.

Personal Mission Statement

- I will base my life on **Love**. My love will conquer my fear.
- I will love, trust, and **respect myself**.
- I will believe I am good enough **on my own**.
- I will love deeply and **hold lightly**.
- I will **always get back up** no matter how many times I fall.
- I will practice **self-discipline**.
- I will **express** my needs and wants . . . again, I will believe that I am **good enough**.
- I will be **proactive** and not just let life happen to me.
- I will be the **heroine** in my story and not the victim.
- I will strive to be **balanced** in all things.
- I will be equally **courageous and considerate** when dealing with people.
- I will remember that **pain is just as important** as happiness, if not more.

- I will be content and grateful for the **present moment**.
- I will trust and follow my **intuition** and gut instincts.
- I will love and I will get hurt, but I will **still love**.

Discovering the Wisdom in My Fear

Fear: Learn to understand what it is and how to harness it.

When we embrace our humanity, we experience divinity.

Six invisible forces that control our lives — six human needs.

1) Need for certainty — people get this from God, bank account, routine, relationships.

2) Need for uncertainty — the unknown, surprises, variety.

These two needs are polar opposites. The dance between certainty and uncertainty is where most people get stuck. Too much in either direction could be unhealthy. Choose the middle path. We have to learn to deal with our emotional response to uncertainty.

3) Need for significance. Feeling important or unique.

4) Need for love and connection. Most people settle for connection because love is too scary.

True love is a humble, powerful force. Love and significance are polar opposites as well. It is all about the dance here as well. Balancing. By being more loving, I become more significant.

These needs will be met in positive or negative ways. The key is to get these needs met with healthy habits.

Last two needs are needs of the spirit:

5) Need for growth. We are either growing or dying. Growing takes time.

6) Need for contribution, to be of service. This is the key to sustainable happiness and cash flow. You are compensated financially to the same degree to which you meet the needs of other people.

Make it your intention to uplift and inspire in any way.

How much uncertainty can I comfortably live with? The quality of my life is directly related to the amount of necessary uncertainty that I can comfortably live with. Question to ask: If I were on my death bed, would I regret not doing this?

Who is making the decisions in your life? The fearful part of yourself or higher self?

Top three times I felt empowered in my life via my subconscious:

- Giving speeches in high school.
- Giving birth with no medication (labor in birthing tub).
- Recording voice-overs.

I felt empowered in my core.

Build spiritual and emotional fitness. We are never going to transcend fear, we must use fear as fuel. Constant growth = uncertainty. I will do the things I love because I have to. I'm going to be afraid, but I'm going to do it anyway because I HAVE TO!

I must experience temporary despair to experience long-term pleasure. Once we master the emotional response to the uncertainty, the logistics are a breeze. Embrace short-term pain to experience long-term pleasure.

Notes from Mastin Kipp's online class.

Beauty

Beauty is everywhere here.
It is in the flickering of a candle,
In the chill of the night air on my neck.
It is in the sweat on my stomach,
And in the sweet sound of the sitar.
Beauty is in the brilliant colors of the
    sunset,
In the smallest detail of a single tree.
It is in the middle place between the
    extremes,
In the territory of love and acceptance.
Beauty rises up from the earth and
    covers me here.
It takes my breath away,
And then gives it back.
Beauty is in the struggle between Love
    and Fear.
It is in the conquering and being
    conquered,
In the pain of defeat and in the joy of
    overcoming.
It is in my sober dance of joy,

Careless, open, and free. Boundless.
Beauty is in sweet smiles from strangers,
And the prepared food plucked straight
     from the earth.
Beauty lies under our programmed
     responses and judgments.
Beauty settles deeper.
Beauty is what I see when I get a
     glimpse of the real you,
And when I allow you to see the real me.
Beauty is all around me here.

Written during a solitary retreat at Esalen.

Collateral Damage

my sweet ten-year-old son was up for two hours last night sobbing his eyes out. He is full of so much pain and sadness. I sat there, my heart breaking for him, breaking for the loss of innocence, breaking for his rude awakening into the pain of life. He expressed his hurt over the divorce, his worry about what he was going to do for a living, his pain of not having his same friends from his old school, his frustration with how humans destroy nature and the environment, his dislike of being crammed into his little desk at school and feeling caged in, his desire for independence, and on and on.

I held him and dried his tears and kissed his cheeks, and inside I felt like death. The weight of his suffering landed straight at my feet, and all I could do was sit there and hold him tight and listen. As painful as it was, my hope is that my son will always come to me when he's suffering, when he's twelve, when he's twenty, when he's fifty.

Sleep tight, son, and know that your mom will always be your candle on the water.

The Run

there I was attempting my first self-motivated three-mile run on the bike trail. I found myself uncomfortable, tired already, and thinking about when I was going to see the mile and a half marker where I could turn around and go back. Then suddenly it dawned on me. Oh right, this was perhaps what they're talking about when they say it's all about the journey and not the destination. My focus was off. My focus was the finish line, the destination.

In that instant, something in my brain shifted and it became about the run, about the air in my face, the clouds in the sky, the twinge in my knee, and the struggle of finding my breath. It became about embracing the entirety of the run, the beauty and the pain, the power and the weakness.

Just as I was accepting these truths and getting more comfortable with the run, a biker waved to me and yelled, "Careful, coyote ahead," as he zipped on by. I slowed down and contemplated walking the rest of the way so that I could watch for the animal, my heart beating quicker, acknowledging the possible danger, but I decided that I was not going to let the unknown, this looming danger, deter me from this goal that I had committed myself to. So I ran a little bit faster.

And so this is life. As soon as we make it about the journey and start accepting it all, a biker comes by to warn us of impending danger or the coyote just comes out of nowhere and mauls us. There is always a possible danger, behind every door and around every corner. The fear can paralyze us and negatively impact our journey, or it can be conquered by action. I plan to just keep running.

Marathon

i am running in my first marathon tomorrow. I decided to run it because I wanted to prove to myself that my body and mind could go to that next level, that I was capable of what I once thought myself incapable of accomplishing, and that little by little I could train my body to do what I needed it to do while wrestling in my mind with the notion that quitting was an option.

The only other time I remember pushing my mind and body in this way was when I gave birth to my son. I opted for the drug-free path and pushed my body and mind WAY out of their comfort zone. The pain was excruciating, but the reward was indescribably fulfilling and valuable.

So ten years later, I am choosing to test my endurance, pain tolerance, and determination once again. Wish me luck! And I will send you all my love and support in whatever "marathon" you're going through in your own life.

Chasing Greatness

about three months ago I joined Toastmasters for the first time ever, and I was so excited. I gave my first get-to-know-me ice breaker speech and that went pretty well. Then it came time to give my second speech.

I'm about a minute into my second speech. For a split second my mind gets distracted from my message and I start focusing of what everyone is thinking about me. And that's when it happens. I start shaking a little bit and then more and then more and then more, until all of a sudden it looks like I'm having a full-blown seizure up on stage. I grasp the podium for support, and as I do that my papers fall to the ground. I bend down to pick them up, and I'm pretty sure I say a cuss word at that point. I get back up, I continue my speech, and eventually the shaking subsides.

When talking to someone who was there and witnessed it afterwards, he told me that he had never seen anything like it before in his life. That's how intense the shaking was. Now, was it one of the most embarrassing things that's ever happened to me? Yes, absolutely. But do you know why I stayed and shook and looked like a fool?

Because I am chasing greatness. There is greatness inside me, and there is so much greatness inside you. We just have to learn how to tap into it, to get beyond the fear that holds us back.

What causes these fears in the first place?

Life. Circumstances. Events out of our control. Conditioning and programming instilled in us as children.

I have three main fears based on some of my life experiences. They are fear of abandonment, fear of rejection, and fear of failure.

1) Fear of abandonment. My parents left for a month-long trip without me when I was six. No letters, no calls. I still remember pacing anxiously and sobbing in my grandma's room as I thought to myself, "They've left me and I'm alone. I'm all alone."

2) Fear of rejection. I remember being chased down the track by three girls in junior high school trying to pants me. I would NOT let go of my pants, so instead they ripped the banana clip out of my hair, along with a good chunk of my actual hair.

3) Fear of failure. I was a finalist in a high school speech contest that was worth a $3,000 scholarship,

and I completely forgot my lines halfway through. I stood there for a solid minute before any words came to me at all. I lost the speech contest and lost the scholarship.

I'm sure each of you has fears based on different events in your lives. But regardless of where these fears came from, I am confident that we can overcome them so that we can continue to chase after greatness. How do we overcome our fears? By facing them. Each and every one of them. By looking at them and talking about them. And then by taking ACTION. We have to do things to prove to ourselves that we are more powerful than our fears.

Instead of allowing that speaking failure that happened twenty years ago to paralyze me, I made a mental decision to get back up and speak again, if for no other reason than to prove to myself that I could do it, that this fear would not have control over me.

So if I have to shake uncontrollably or throw up or cry or forget my lines while giving a speech, I'll do it over and over and over again. Because I am chasing greatness. Won't you please join me?

A speech given for an audition for Kevin Bracy's MonSTARS of Motivation Show.

Deeper Places

How much love is in my heart?
How much wisdom can I gain?
How much time do I have left?
How much insight falls like rain?
How many lives can I improve?
How many souls can my soul touch?
How many wounds can my love cure?
How many days, oh please, how much?
This time goes by so fast,
Soon enough, one breath, my last.
Fully I will live right now,
With passion I will work and plow.
My vision and my purpose clear,
To love and love, despite the fear.
To see way past the programmed mind,
To deeper places, I'm sure I'll find.
For you and I, large or small
Are perfect creatures, beneath it all.

What I Want

❧ I want to create enough love and completeness in my being that I never again have to look outside of myself to find my own worth and value.

❧ I want to continue taming my thoughts to dwell on the positive, to be forever grateful, and to take responsibility for my life.

❧ I want to always listen to and trust my intuition.

❧ I want to help others who struggle with low self-esteem and self-worth to know how beautiful they really are.

❧ I want to evolve more and more in the four areas of life: mental, emotional, physical, and spiritual. And I want to be balanced in all of them.

❧ I want to continue taking steps toward the woman that I know I am: confident, loving, powerful, giving, caring, bold, peaceful, self-assured, and self-defined.

❧ I want to truly love people without judgment and without expectation.

- I want to be aware of the fear and judgment that I do have and see what those thoughts are telling me about myself and where I need to grow.
- I want to prove to myself that all the limits that I believe are there are actually self-imposed and can be crossed over.
- I want to write about life and personal growth and present speeches based on my writings.
- I want to rise above and I want to do it for the sake of Love.

Grateful

I am grateful for good people.

I am grateful for true friends and deep conversations.

I am grateful for God and the mystery of what that even means.

I am grateful for pain and for relief.

I am grateful for challenges and obstacles.

I am grateful for peace and tranquility.

I am grateful for endings and for beautiful beginnings.

I am grateful for the fight and am grateful for the rest.

I am grateful for laughter that soothes my soul.

I am grateful for iced coffee on a hot day.

I am grateful for surprises on my doorstep.

I am grateful for a dog who loves me regardless.

I am grateful for tears cried and tears dried.

I am grateful for plans and goals.

I am grateful for the present moment.

I am grateful that I don't have to have all the
  answers.
I am grateful when I can embrace it all . . .
The ups and downs, the rain and the rays,
  the dark and the light,
The uncertainty and the conviction, the past
  and the unknown future.
I am grateful for life.

The Beginning of an Unfinished Book

i close my eyes because everything I know and want to write about lies deep inside me. If anything, it's my fears and worries that get in the way, and I am done listening to those. So I sit here with my eyes closed at about 9 a.m. on a Tuesday morning. I close my eyes because it allows me to focus on the voice inside of me that is small and soft, but longs to be heard. It is the voice that matters above all, and I silence that voice far too easily. I am convinced now that I silence her because I do not know her well yet. I do not fully trust her yet. But just because she is unfamiliar does not mean that she is not safe.

I have dropped my kids off at school and I sit here with a blank page in front of me and years of experiences, thoughts, and feelings surging inside me. I can hear my dog moving around on the couch. It's a sunny day today. Spring is in full swing. It's been a little over a year since the divorce finalized, and two years since the separation. I am still figuring out my life. As I think back on it, I realize how everything that happened and all of the choices that I made have led me to this specific moment, sitting here, alone, on a bright sunny day in April, writing about deep loss and deeper love.

Ready

Ready to live.
Ready to be all that I was meant to be.
Ready to step out and up and beyond.
Ready to do it all despite the fear.
Ready to take off the masks and truly be.
Ready to surrender to the power inside of me.
Ready to let go . . . of worry, of fear, of pain.
Ready to live free of judgment and hypocrisy.
Ready to show love, to be love.
Are you ready too?

About the Author

Janice Angela Burt is a court-certified Spanish interpreter, a voice-over artist, and an inspirational speaker. She lives in Sacramento, California, with her two adorable children and her dog, Copper. Visit her online at spanishjanice.com.

CPSIA information can be obtained at www.ICGtesting.com
Printed in the USA
BVOW08s1601181113

336574BV00001B/1/P

9 780989 912518